DIDGERIDOO

A COMPLETE GUIDE TO THIS ANCIENT ABORIGINAL INSTRUMENT

A Playing Instruction Manual

For The Beginner To The Advanced Player

BY JOHN BOWDEN

First published 1994
John P. Bowden

P.O. Box 508 Kallangur,
Queensland, 4503
Australia.
Design, Text, and Artwork by
John P. Bowden.

JOHN P. BOWDEN
P.O. BOX 595
ALBANY CREEK, Q. 4035

FAX: (07) 3264 3921
EMAIL:
john@didgeridoo-australia.com
WEBSITE:
www.didgeridoo-australia.com

National Library of Australia
Card Number ISBN 0 646 22586 3

FOREWORD

John Bowden excels as both a teacher and musician. With over thirty years experience in both fields, he is well respected by students and colleages alike. John has successfully taught didgeridoo to students ranging from the ages of seven to seventy and of varying ability.

Brought up in the bush in the upper Brisbane Valley, John spent much of his early teaching career in Camooweal, a small town west of Mt. Isa. He was later transferred to Sandgate High, where he taught maths, science, earth science and biology. It was here that John became an integral part of school life in academic, cultural and sporting arenas. His retirement in 1993 was mourned by countless students.

As a musician, John worked in South-east Queensland in local Brisbane bands from the sixties through to the eighties as a vocalist and guitarist. John taught guitar as well as the blues harmonica which he also plays.

An active supporter of several environmental projects, John has even established a rainforest on his own property at Albany Creek, where he resides with his wife, Glenda. Here, he breeds native Australian birds, and is a nationally regarded authority on the subject.

His experience teaching didgeridoo to school groups and adult education classes, his comprehensive knowledge of the Australian bush, together with his investigations into Aboriginal culture combine successfully to produce a manual for didgeridoo that is both 'user-friendly' and informative.

Kim Anderson

Kim Anderson B.A.(Mus), A. Mus. A., B.Ed. St.,
Grad. Dip. Teach. Mus.
Instrumental Music Coordinator,
Sandgate District State High School.

ACKNOWLEDGEMENTS

Sincere thanks must go to: Graham and Robert, and to Kim, for their help and advice in the production of this book; to my wife for her tolerance and patience; to my students who have provided feedback as to what interested them and what worked for them; and to the many people (Aboriginal and non-Aboriginal) who have helped me to learn more about the didgeridoo over the years. Andres Segovia once said that you can never master the guitar. Alan Dargin said the same of the didgeridoo. We are all still learning.

John Bowden

About This Book

Until now, as far as I know, there have been only a few books available on didgeridoo - and these have been mere introductions. Here, for the first time, I believe, is a complete manual which will enable the keen student to become a proficient player.

This book is divided into six chapters. Each chapter contains one lesson on the art of playing didgeridoo. As well, in each chapter, there is information about the didgeridoo, its origin, its manufacture, Aboriginal culture, and other related topics which I feel are necessary to give the didgeridoo player and owner a better appreciation of this intriguing instrument.

The chapters and lessons become progressively longer, but not necessarily more difficult. The length of time required for each lesson will depend on your previous playing experience and the success you achieve as you progress. In general, later lessons will require more time and study. Ways of creating new sounds or combinations of sounds are suggested so that you may develop your own style. Previous lessons should be revised when difficulties arise.

To The Didgeridoo Teacher

For the beginning students, Lessons 1 and 2 should take about an hour each, and you, the teacher, should explain and demonstrate each step. A week for practice should follow each lesson.

Lesson 3 can be introduced whether the student has mastered circular breathing or not. Recordings of the actual calls of animals (such as birds) are available from environmental shops. It really creates interest and assists the students if the calls described in this chapter (and other calls suitable for imitation on the didgeridoo) are played and then demonstrated by the teacher prior to attempts by students.

Lessons 4, 5 and 6 may each be taught as two or more lessons of one hour duration, depending on the progress of the students or the class, or on the circumstances. Lesson 6, especially, may require several one hour sessions separated by time for practice. The exercises and practical studies in lessons 4, 5 and 6 are open to a wide degree of interpretation by you, the tutor. There is also much scope for you to extend each lesson with your own ideas. One of the main intentions of these later chapters is to encourage experimentation and individuality in the students.

CONTENTS

Dioscorea transversa (Long Yam)

INTRODUCTION

In recent years there has been a tremendous upsurge of interest in the didgeridoo. Especially since 1988, the bicentenial year of the first permanent settlement of Europeans in Australia, there has been an ever-increasing awareness of things Australian, not only by people from overseas, but by Australians themselves. And this is well overdue.

The sound of the didgeridoo is somehow quintessential to the very soul of Australia's natural landscape. No other sound can evoke memories and images of the Australian outback better than the haunting tones of the didgeridoo. And what Australian does not like to think that he or she has an affinity with the bush?

The didgeridoo is to Australia, what the bagpipes are to Scotland, what the steel guitar and ukelele are to Hawaii, what the sitar is to India, the Flamenco guitar to Spain, and the mandolin to Italy. Unlike the instruments of these other countries however, the didgeridoo had its origin and development entirely within the country with which it is now associated.

This book, '*Didgeridoo*', provides a complete guide to the playing of this ancient instrument. Also included is background information so that the reader and prospective didgeridooist can appreciate the importance of the didgeridoo to the Aborigines for whom it was, and still is, part of social and ceremonial life, and who have bequethed the joy of hearing and playing this fascinating wind instrument to other Aborigines, and other fellow Australians; and to the rest of the world.

A great deal of pleasure can be had in playing the didgeridoo. Indeed, it can be great fun just trying. Once you are only a little proficient at it, you can have fun with others, say at a party, if you bring out your didge, and several pieces of 40mm P.V.C. pipe (to which you have moulded bees wax mouth-pieces) for them to have a try.

When you have mastered circular breathing, you have a great opportunity to practice very effective relaxation techniques. This is because of the deep and controlled breathing involved, and your concentration on the sounds you are creating.

CHAPTER 1

THE DIDGERIDOO

The didgeridoo (didjeridu, didgiridoo, ditjeridoo, etc.) is an ancient instrument of music, played by the Australian Aborigines. It is not the oldest musical instrument of the world - humans have probably made music from the earliest times, using pieces of rock, wood, or bone struck together; slivers of wood or stretched string plucked; hollow logs or bamboo pieces hit with sticks; and pipes of reed, bamboo, or cattle horn blown.

Origin

It has been estimated that the age of the earliest use of the didgeridoo was less than two thousand years ago. This relatively recent time has been calculated by estimating how long it would have taken for knowledge of it to have spread from its place of origin to the places where it is known to have been in use when Europeans came into contact with Aborigines in these regions. The didgeridoo was part of the culture, in these times, only in the northern areas of the Northern Territory and in the north-eastern parts of the Kimberleys, of Western Australia.

The approximate distribution of the didgeridoo in traditional Aboriginal culture.
(Compare with the distribution of Eucalyptus tetrodonta on page 4.)

Recently, of course, Aboriginal and non-Aboriginal Australians from all parts of Australia have taken an interest in the didgeridoo as a serious musical instrument, as a curiosity, as a symbol of Australian culture, as a work of art, or as a decoration and talking point for the rumpus room or bar. A didgeridoo is becoming a must for overseas tourists to take home as a momento of their Australian visit. And what could be a more suitable token of Australia ?

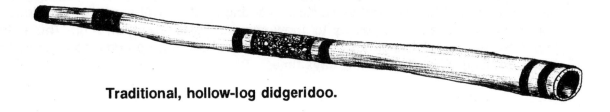

Traditional, hollow-log didgeridoo.

A Didgeridoo For Beginners

If you are planning to learn to play the didgeridoo, you may not wish to outlay a lot of money. A good wooden didgeridoo, even one that is not decorated, will, most likely, cost in the hundreds of dollars. A good starter's didge can be made from P.V.C. waste-water pipe. Warm some bee's wax, fashion a mouth-piece from it at one end, and you are ready to start. A piece of 40mm P.V.C. pipe 1.19 metres long will produce a D pitch.

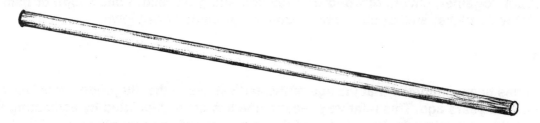

P.V.C. pipe didgeridoo, suitable for beginning 'didgeridooists'.

Playing The Didgeridoo - Lesson 1.

Before you start, remember, it takes time and patience to learn anything new and difficult, and every person is different - each person finds different skills easier or harder to acquire than other people do. Persistent practice will definitely pay dividends; so work on it. Don't give up. Also remember, when you are first starting (and maybe later as well) other people are not going to be as keen as you are on the various sounds that you will be creating, so be considerate, lock yourself away in the wood shed or in your room until you have mastered your art to a point where others will be impressed with what you do, at least at first. Just think, soon you will be the life of every party.

Let's do it !

1. Making the basic droning sound - the fundamental.

This is done by vibrating your lips loosely, while pressing them lightly into the mouth-piece - like blowing a raspberry or making the noise that horses typically make with their lips. Not the big end, Silly, the end with the smaller opening, maybe fashioned from bees wax - the mouth-piece. Some people use the front of their mouth while playing the didgeridoo, while others prefer to use one side. Whatever method suits you is correct.

Having trouble? It is probably because you are trying too hard. Loosen up; your lips especially. Think low and slow. If you still have not got that rich, didgeridoo droning sound (and you will know when you have got it because you will feel the didge vibrate), try to make the sound of your vibrating lips go continually down in pitch until you hit the note. It is there somewhere for everybody. If you cannot find it, try going up in pitch - you may be one of the few who start too low and slow. Keep working on it - it will come to you. Notice, when you think you have it, and you try to show someone else, you muff it up. This is because you tense up. Right? Hang loose. Soon it will be second nature - you won't know how you could not have done it - in a few days time.

2. Those eerie tone changes

It is the tone changes that give the **didgeridoo** its haunting sound, and mystical appeal. Now that you can produce the fundamental droning sound (even if you have not quite mastered it yet), you can begin to make some interesting changes to its tone. This is done by changing the shape of your lips on the mouth-piece. As you drone, shape your mouth as if you are slowly saying, 'Oooeee-Oooeee' , without using your voice - the tone of the fundamental will change from 'smooth' to 'nasal'. As you do this, you may notice that your tongue moves from further back on the floor of your mouth (on 'ooo') up to the base of your lower teeth (on 'eee'). Be patient, it will not be easy at first to keep your droning sound going while you change the tone. Soon however, you will find it a breeze.

Having got this change of tone going , try to speed up the tone changes, or slow them down. That is, do a fast 'oooeee -oooeee' and a slow one. Do a loud one and a soft one. You can also change the tone of these two basic tones. For example, while you are doing the 'eee' tone (the nasal fundamental), keep your tongue up against your lower teeth and change the shape of your lips as if saying, 'Wee-wee-wee-' etc. Similary, make the 'ooo' tone (the smooth fundamental), keeping the tongue back on the floor of your mouth as you shape your lips as if saying, 'You-you-you-' etc. Notice how the back of your tongue moves up and down.

Now that you have these 'oooeee-oooeee' tone changes going, try to make some explosive 'wok, wok' sounds by forcing the change of tone from 'ooo' to 'eee' . Make the 'ooo' tone and then shape your mouth as if to say, 'Ooo-Wee' . Hear the 'Wok' sound as you do this suddenly, emphasizing the 'wa' sound produced.

Confused? Don't worry, it does not matter. The whole point here is to make as many variations as possible on the droning sound. Listen to other players and try to copy their tone changes - adapt these to suit yourself. Invent some of your own.

Some Fun Sounds

(a) The sound of a returning boomerang in flight can be made by using the tone changes we have done. Shape your mouth as if to say, 'Yoiee, Yoiee, ' etc (rhymes with 'toyee') as you drone. Start loudly at first and become softer as the boomerang goes further away. As it returns, increase the volume.

(b) The sound of a kangaroo hopping through the bush can be imitated by shaping your lips as if to pronounce, 'Doiee, Doiee' as you drone. Emphasize the first syllable. Start loudly and slowly at first, then vary the speed and go softer.

(c) The sound of a car approaching and then going past can be achieved by altering the drone sound. Start with a soft drone and, if you can, a slightly lower pitch. Increase the volume and pitch as the car approaches, reaching a peak as it passes. Now drop the volume and pitch of the drone as the car moves into the distance. You physicists will know that this change of pitch an observer hears as a car goes past is called the Doppler effect. But you do not have to know this to do the sound. So who cares ?

CHAPTER 2

The didgeridoo is made from trunks or limbs of trees, hollowed out by certain arboreal species of termite. In the northern parts of Australia, particular species of termite (eg. <u>Coptotermes acinaciformes</u>) live in and eat out the central portions of living trees as well as dead ones, filling the hollow with a mixture of gritty material that they obtain from the soil below, and faecal waste. This mixture contains the tunnels up and down through which the insects travel as they continue to work the wood.

In the less fertile and drier areas of monsoonal regions of the North, almost all of the individual trees that make up some populations of certain Eucalyptus species contain these termites and are hollow. Many could be made into didgeridoos. It is no wonder that the didgeridoo evolved here. Some species of trees used to make didgeridoos include: Eucalyptus ptychocarpa (Swamp Bloodwood), E. tetrodonta (Darwin Stringybark), E. miniata (Darwin Woolybutt) and E. phoenicea (Scarlet Gum). The ranges of the last three species extend into Queensland.

Distribution of Eucalyptus tetrodonta (Darwin Stringybark)[1]

Distribution of Eucalyptus miniata (Darwin Woolybutt)[2]

Making a Didgeridoo

To make a didgeridoo, a suitable trunk or branch is selected by tapping it to see if it is hollow. It is then cut a little longer than will be required and is soaked for a few days in water to soften the termite tunnel-material. Next, the termite material is prised out by use of a thin, hard stick or piece of wire. Slivers of wood on the inside of the hollow have to be removed. These may have to be burnt out. Cracks, knot-holes and borer-holes are then filled with bees wax, and a mouth-piece may be added at the smaller end (using bees wax). The pipe is now sounded and cut to the length which gives the desired pitch.

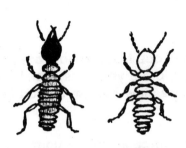

Soldier   Worker
Two castes of termite

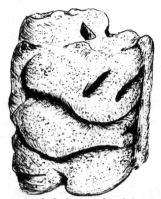

Core-material deposited by termites
in hollowed-out tree trunk or branch.

The pitch (i.e. the highness or lowness of the note) of the didgeridoo depends on the volume of air inside the pipe. For a given diameter, the pitch depends on the length - the longer it is the lower the note; the shorter the length the higher the note. A pipe with a wider inside diameter does not have to be as long to produce a low note. Similarly, a long didgeridoo will not produce as low a note if the hollow inside is not as wide. The shape of the inside hollow and where the air is agitated to produce the sound may also affect the pitch. This can be illustrated by blowing a wooden didgeridoo at the other end - you may find that the pitch is different from that of the sound produced when blown from the opposite end.

Every didgeridoo made of a natural tree trunk or branch is different. Even though they may have the same pitch, because of the different qualities of the wood, the varying widths of the hollow, the differing bends, the differing widths of the walls of the pipe, and the varying surfaces on the inside walls, different didgeridoos have their own unique tonal qualities.

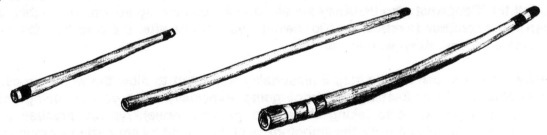

Playing The Didgeridoo - Lesson 2.

Now that you can get the basic droning sound (or even if you can't as yet), it is time to learn the very important technique of circular breathing. This skill is essential if you are to master didgeridoo playing. It is all a matter of mind over body, and though many people at first find it difficult to do (in fact virtually impossible), they soon realise that it is actually very simple and, once mastered, becomes almost second nature. Once again, don't even consider giving up - the next time you attempt it, you may do it. Keep trying. It can take a few minutes to learn the basic skill, or a few hours, or even a few weeks. It is a case of concentrating very hard on the muscles you use for breathing in, and those used in squeezing air out of your puffed-out cheeks.

What we are aiming to do here is to keep the droning sound going - that is, keep your lips vibrating - by using air in your mouth and puffed-out cheeks, while you sniff air in through your nose. Let's try a method of learning circular breathing that I have used successfully to teach many others. Hopefully, it will help you.

Circular Breathing

1. <u>Without the didge</u>: Hold your breath with your cheeks puffed out. Now, without breathing, use your cheek muscles to force air out of your mouth to vibrate your lips. Don't worry about the sound. Do this lots of times, one after another in a slow rhythm as you tap at about one beat per second.

2. <u>Still without the didge</u>: Do as in step 1, but now, as you force air out of your cheeks, sniff air in through your nose at the same time. This will take great concentration at first, so keep trying. Hold your breath before you start forcing the air out of your cheeks. Tapping to keep the rhythm helps your timing.

If you cannot do this step successfully, don't worry. Proceed with step 3.

3. <u>Now use the didgeridoo</u>. Blow a short basic drone of about one second long with your cheeks puffed out as far as you can, and at the end of it, hold your breath and force the air out of your cheeks, as in step 1. The sound as you blow the air from the cheeks will change from the basic drone as you do this. Overall, the resulting sound will be like 'Doowhat'. Do this many times as you tap a slow rhythm with your hand or foot on 'what'.

4. Do as in step 3, but now, as you blow air from your cheeks, sniff air in through your nose. Concentrate. Concentrate on your cheek muscles and your sniffing of air through your nostrils. The sound you should get is like 'Dooowhat; Dooowhat' etc. 'Dooo' is the basic drone and 'what' is the sound as you force air out of your cheeks, and simultaneously, take air in through your nose.

5. If you have managed step 4, you are practically there. All we have to do now is to combine all the 'Dooowhat's so that they are all part of a continuing sound. To do this, do as in step 4, but continue to repeat the 'Dooowhat' sounds, one after the other at a fair rate - about once a second. Keep working on this.

6. Finally, once you can handle step 5 reasonably well, start to slow the whole process down, and concentrate on keeping the drone going, especially when you are using your cheeks (i.e. when you are also taking air in through your nose). As you practise this technique, you can greatly improve the smoothness of the sound by squeezing as much air as possible from your mouth.

If you still find that you cannot join the 'dooo-what' sounds into a continuous drone, try speeding up the whole process, concentrating on your lips, to keep them vibrating during the 'what' part of the cycle.

The volume of air available can be increased by

> (i) inflating the cheeks as much as possible and
> (ii) moving the tongue as far back in the mouth as possible before you start to use the air in your cheeks. The tongue is moved forward as you use air from the cheeks (and breathe in through the nose).

Another technique which will improve the amount of air you have to vibrate your lips, involves the correct use of the diaphragm. The diaphragm is the muscular wall between your chest cavity and your abdominal cavity.

If you consciously move your abdominal ('belly') wall out as you breathe in, and force it in as you do the drone part of the sound, you are probably on the right track. (See page 9)

Once you can circular breathe, you need only take in air through your nose (while you are using your cheek muscles) as you require it, not in a regular pattern, unless you are using the circular breathing as part of a rhythm pattern.

<u>Note</u> : Some people never master circular breathing, because they try too hard. They force it, and attempt to do it all in a great hurry. When it does not happen, they become more and more frustrated. It is not usual for a person to be able to take their first circular breath without first sitting and quietly working through the steps alone. You do not have to sniff hard - just a short, soft breath of air through your nostrils is all you need.

Eucalyptus ptychocarpa   (Swamp Bloodwood)

The Physiology Of Circular Breathing

Study the following diagrams which show how the tongue moves to force air out of the mouth and through the lips to keep them vibrating (as you take air in through your nostrils). This is happening while you are squeezing air out of your cheeks.

Diagram (a) Air (from the lungs) is being blown normally, through the mouth and into the didgeridoo via the vibrating lips. This is what happens when you are playing but not circular breathing, or between circular breaths.

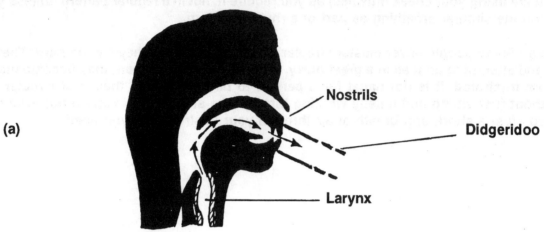

(a)
Nostrils

Didgeridoo

Larynx

Diagram (b) At the start of the circular breath, the tongue is raised up at the back of the mouth, ready to force air, trapped in the mouth, out through the lips and into the didgeridoo. The player is now starting to sniff air in through the nostrils.

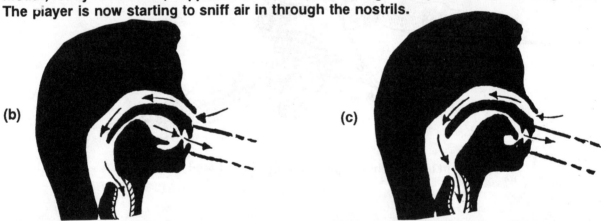

(b)

(c)

Diagram (c) At the end of the circular breath, the tongue has moved forward to push the air out of the mouth, through the lips, and into the didgeridoo. Air has now been taken into the lungs via the nose. The player now uses this air to blow normally through the didge, as in diagram (a).

Now if you cannot follow any of this, it does not mean that you will not be able to circular breathe. In fact, for some people, the more they think about controlling certain muscles, the less control they seem to have.

Just keep working quietly with yourself: you'll do it.

Increasing your Air Capacity

Once you can circular breathe, you will be able to sustain a continuous drone for a long time. However, to be able to play strongly for hours while doing various sounds that require a large output of air, you need to develop your capacity to do this. Generally, the more you play, the better this capacity improves. However, to help increase your ability to perform powerful fills while you continue to drone, you should become aware of the function of the diaphragm in breathing technique.

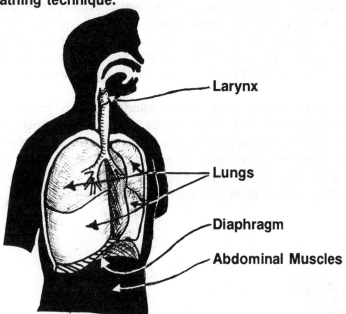

To enable us to breathe in, the rib-cage is raised up and out and the diaphragm is lowered. This increases the volume within the thoracic (chest) cavity, thus lowering the pressure. The pressure of air in the atmosphere causes air to flow into the lungs where the pressure is less. To breathe out, the rib-cage is forced down and in while the diaphragm is raised. This decreases the volume inside the thoracic cavity, making the pressure inside it greater than atmospheric pressure, forcing air out.

If you want to take a lot of air in quickly, the diaphragm has to be lowered as far as possible while the rib-cage is being raised. To assist the lowering of the diaphragm, the abdominal ('tummy') wall has to be moved outwards. To blow the maximum amount of air out of the lungs, the diaphragm can be forced upwards by moving the abdominal wall inwards as you blow. So to sustain a long blown-note, use your diaphragm by pushing in gradually with your abdominal wall.

To produce a burst of air for an explosive sound, the diaphragm can be pushed upwards quickly by sudden contractions of your abdominal-wall muscles. This is what happens when you cough or sneeze. Put you hand on your abdomen, cough, and feel what happens. As you breathe in, during circular breaths, your abdomen should move outwards. You may be doing the opposite to this. Change it, to play more powerfully.

Deeper breathing, associated with the proper use of your diaphragm as you breathe, is very relaxing. It can help lower your blood pressure and decrease your heart rate.

In short, **playing the didgeridoo is good for you !**

CHAPTER 3

Traditional Didgeridoo

Because Aboriginal groups did not stay very long in one place, but moved onto new hunting and camping grounds periodically, most instruments used for making music were not carried from place to place. Instead, they were often renewed at the new camp. A new didgeridoo was readily constructed when required, since the materials needed for manufacture were often close at hand. However, particularly good instruments and those used for sacred ceremonies, would be kept and secreted away in safe places - hollow trees or logs, or in caves or rock crevices - to be used again when the group returned.

The best instruments were often handed down from father to son for many generations. The decorations on didgeridoos included paintings, produced by application of natural ochres, and engraving, initially done by use of stoneknives and gravers, and more recently by using glass or steel tools. Often the decorations were very simple, if used at all. Sacred instruments and those kept for any length of time would be decorated, the ornamentation being added to or gone over from time to time.

Stone knife: used for carving decorations.

Woomera: a spear thrower, used also as a graver for inscribing decorations.

Playing The Didgeridoo - Lesson 3.

In this lesson, we are going to add other sounds to the basic droning of the didgeridoo - all at the same time - amazing!

If at this stage you can circular breathe, great, but if you can't, it does not matter - keep working on it and eventually you'll do it. For now though, all of the skills in this lesson can be done with or without circular breathing.

1. Animal Sounds.

The following sounds are made simply by using your larynx (your voice box) as you do for normal speech - either in a falsetto (squeeky) fashion or a normal high or low pitch, depending on the required sounds - while at the same time maintaining the drone note. To assist you in producing some of these imitations in an authentic way, you should listen carefully to the real sounds, from life or from recorded sounds.

Let's now try some truly Australian sounds.

Boobook Owl - this is Australia's smallest but most observed owl. It is still found in some well-treed, suburban areas, and is often called 'mopoke' because of the sound it makes. Get your drone sound going and at the same time speak the words 'oak koke' in a falsetto voice, the first syllable higher than the second. Repeat every three or so seconds.

Southern Boobook Owl

Laughing Kookaburra - everybody knows the call of this bird. Simply do a whole lot of falsetto 'kook, kook, kook' sounds with rising and falling pitch, etc., as you keep the drone going.

Laughing Kookaburra

Bar-shouldered Dove - this graceful pigeon is being displaced by the introduced Spotted Turtle-dove, but can still be found in scrubby country around towns, and in less-altered areas. It occurs over most of eastern and northern Australia. It's sound is like 'Hook-a-wook, Hook-a-wook', and the whole of this is repeated after a space of about two seconds before the next call. Say it into the didge in a high falsetto voice.

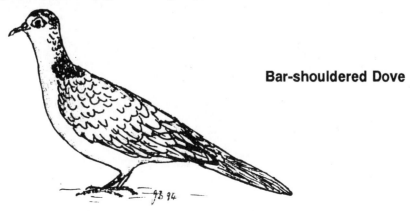

Bar-shouldered Dove

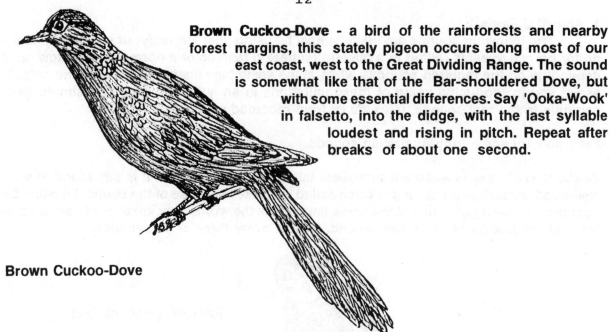

Brown Cuckoo-Dove - a bird of the rainforests and nearby forest margins, this stately pigeon occurs along most of our east coast, west to the Great Dividing Range. The sound is somewhat like that of the Bar-shouldered Dove, but with some essential differences. Say 'Ooka-Wook' in falsetto, into the didge, with the last syllable loudest and rising in pitch. Repeat after breaks of about one second.

Brown Cuckoo-Dove

Peaceful Dove - this beautiful, little dove occurs over most of eastern, northern and central Australia. It has a high-pitched call like 'Ooeeook'. Say this into the didge with your highest falsetto voice. It also makes a trilling sound which can be done on the didgeridoo by using a technique called 'flutter tongueing' as you do a high-pitched 'trrooo' sound, falling in pitch. To flutter tongue, place the tip of your tongue on the roof of your mouth, and make it flutter as you blow air over it. You probably used this method when you were small, to imitate a motor bike. The ability to flutter tongue may be genetically acquired, which means that if you cannot do it, you never will. But don't despair, later on we will learn a technique anyone can do which produces a similar effect.

Peaceful Dove

Torresian Imperial-Pigeon

Torresian Imperial Pigeon - this large pigeon occurs in coastal parts of northern Australia. The sounds are like 'Ook-Wooo' and 'Wooo', with the pitch falling. Do this in low falsetto.

Pheasant Coucal - this pheasant-like, long, brown bird occurs over most of eastern and northern Australia. Its call can be mimicked by droning while voicing the following sounds, in a low falsetto: 'Coo-Coo-Coo-Coo-Coo-Coo-Coo- Coo-Coo—Coo-Coo-Coo-Coo-Coo'. The first eight or so 'Coo's are equally spaced and falling in pitch, and the last six or so rise in pitch and get faster.

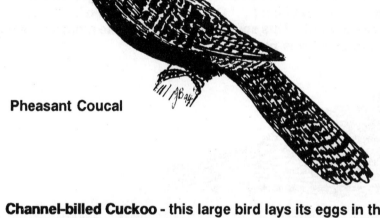

Pheasant Coucal

Channel-billed Cuckoo - this large bird lays its eggs in the nests of crows, currawongs, and similar birds. It can be heard over most of northern and eastern Australia during the warmer months. Its calls are loud and raucous. Say the followinginto the didge in falsetto - the first series of notes getting progressively higher in pitch, the last ones starting fast and getting slower as they decrease in pitch. 'Kor, Kor, Kor, Kor, Kor, Kor, Kook-Kook-Kook-Kook-Kook-Kook-Kook'. A touch of insanity helps here.

Channel-billed Cuckoo

Tawny Frogmouth - this nocturnal bird, which is not an owl, occurs over all of Australia. It makes a sound like a didgeridoo - like 'Om-Oomm' repeated monotonously, as well as a higher series of repeated 'Oo' sounds. To imitate it, make a series of low 'Er-Eerr' sounds in your normal voice, about a second apart, then some fairly low falsetto 'Oo' sounds, about two a second, before returning to the lower calls again.

Tawny Frogmouth

White-throated Nightjar - also called Nighthawk, and a relative of the Tawny Frogmouth, this nocturnal, small bird makes an eerie call, which sounds good on the didgeridoo. You imitate it by doing the following in high falsetto voice, the notes after the first couple, getting faster and faster, and higher in pitch: 'Ook-Kook-Kook-Kook-Kook-Kook-Kook-Kook-Kook-Kook-Kook- Kook'. This sounds like a two-stroke motor-mower engine as it fails to start when the starter cord is pulled.

White-throated Nightjar

Pied or Magpie Goose - this large wading bird, found mainly in the north and north-east of Australia, once occurred in immense populations even as far south as Victoria. The call is a loud honking, which can be imitated on the didgeridoo by making a high-pitched falsetto sound like 'teernt-teernt-teernt-teernt .....'. This call is good for ventriloquial effects. Imitate the geese coming towards you by starting softly and then increasing the volume and pitch, or have them flying away as they call by starting loudly and then lowering the pitch and volume.

Pied or Magpie Goose

Barking Dog - this can be done in either falsetto or normal voice by saying a low,'Ruff, Ruff', or a falsetto, 'Oo, Oo', into the didge as you continue to drone. These give you big and little dogs respectively.

Howling Dingo - a falsetto 'Oooooooo, Oo Oo, Ooooooooo' trailing downwards will give you a good dingo howl with yelping in between. Dingoes don't bark.

Dingo

Once you can handle these examples, increase your repertoire by listening - to other players during live performances and on recordings, to recordings of animal calls, but especially to the sounds of nature all around us. Go bush just to listen - at dawn, during the day and at night. Different environments have different sounds - be observant and creative. Some sounds work well on the didgeridoo while others are not suitable. However, the possibilities are almost limitless.

2. Ventriloquial Effects.

Interesting variations can be produced with the above sounds, and others you may create yourself, if you give the impression that the sound is coming from near by or from far away. You do this by changing the shape of your mouth and its position in the mouthpiece.

To get a near sound, spread your lips more on the mouthpiece - like when you smile - and do not press them as hard on it while you do your imitation. Or, you can turn your head slightly to one side on the mouth-piece as you do the close-up sound. You have to be careful, while doing these close-up sounds, not to lose the drone.

To make it sound as if the call is coming from further away, force your lips further into the pipe and make their shape more rounded.Of course, sounds that are far away do not sound as loud, so make these softer (the imitation that is, not the drone - keep this at a constant volume).

Make your imitations of closer sounds louder. You can give the impression of a sound coming towards you,or moving into the distance, by use of these techniques. e.g. a bird which calls as it flies away, or calls as it comes closer, can be imitated.

3. Double Notes and Chords.

You can make the didgeridoo play two notes at once. You do this by singing or humming sounds such as 'Oooo' or 'Aaaa' as you produce the drone note. This can be the same pitch as, or a different pitch from the drone note. Thus you can produce harmonies (chords) by singing the note a third (or 10th) or a fifth (12th) higher than the drone note.This means that the note you sing has a pitch the same as the third or fifth note in the scale, taking the drone note as being the first note of the scale. (Actually these added voiced notes are probably one or two octaves higher than the true pitch of the drone note - but let's not be too technical).

You can also sing the equivalent notes lower than the drone note. The notes we are talking about here are the ones in the major chord - the 'mi' and 'so' of 'do, mi, so, do'. 'Do' is the note played by the drone of the didgeridoo - the fundamental. Other notes of the scale can also be sung or hummed with the drone note to produce different effects. For example, sevenths, minor sevenths, sixths, augmented fifths, fourths, minor thirds, and seconds, but these may sound harsh. You will get different effects if you sing in your normal voice or your falsetto voice. You can make the didgeridoo produce interesting growling effects by singing low notes of certain pitches while you drone. By gargling in a low pitch at the back of your throat, you can produce a sound similar to that of a flutter tongue. Vary the pitch to find the best effect.

Experiment with these techniques of singing in unison with the drone, to invent your own special effects. However, you will find that you can only make these extra notes as you exhale, and between each inhalation as you circular breathe. With this technique you can also reproduce novelty sounds such as revving trucks, cars and motor bikes - complete with gear changes, as well as planes and sirens.

Eucalyptus phoenicea (Scarlet Gum)

CHAPTER 4

Didgeridoo Decorations

These days, the didgeridoos one sees for sale are often ornately decorated - they are virtual works of art, in vinyl or oil paints. Too often they are colourful and glossy to such an extent that they have lost the natural beauty for which Aboriginal works, done in the ochre colours of Australia, have become world famous.

The paint used by Aborigines for decorating didgeridoos and other objects was made from minerals obtained from rocks and soils which originated by weathering processes over millions of years. Australia is particularly rich in minerals such as haematite, limonite and bauxite, that occur in laterite deposits which are produced under intense monsoonal conditions - the conditions which occurred over the northern two-thirds of the Australian continent during the Miocene epoch (about 15 million years ago). The far north of Australia still has this type of climate. Haematite yields red and brown ochres, limonite reds, browns and yellows, and bauxite grey, yellow, white and even dull blue.

Extent (approx.)of Miocene monsoonal climate.

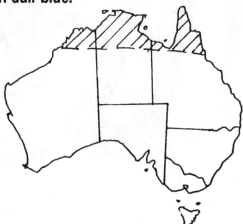

Extent (approx.) of present monsoonal climate.

Rounded, partially-hollow rocks, called ironstone concretions, often contain a mixture of all of these minerals, and were much prized and traded by the Aborigines. In some places minerals such as malachite (green) and azurite (blue), derived from copper bearing rocks, were mined. Black was obtained from charcoal and sometimes manganese dioxide (pyrolusite). Clay minerals (such as bauxite and kaolinite) and gypsum were used for white.

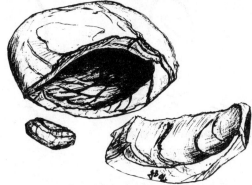

Cut-away diagram of a hollow, ironstone concretion showing concentric layers and loose ochre material.

To make paint, Aborigines powdered rock, soil or mineral and mixed it with water or natural fixatives such as orchid sap, emu fat, turtle eggs, honey or wax. It was applied by use of a chewed, plant-stem brush, or feathers, by using the fingers, or via the mouth. These days, Aboriginal artists may still use these ochres but often they are mixed with water and modern, water-soluble glues.

Motifs used commonly in decorations include food animals such as fish, marsupials (kangaroos, bandicoots, etc), monotremes (echidna, platypus), reptiles (snakes, lizards, tortoises, etc.) birds, etc., as well as human figures and mythical beings. Plants sometimes feature in paintings, as do tracks, pathways and natural geological phenomena such as water holes, streams, and rocks, usually represented by symbols.

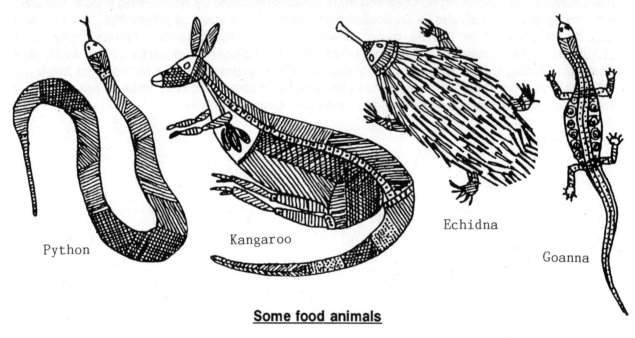

Python Kangaroo Echidna Goanna

Some food animals

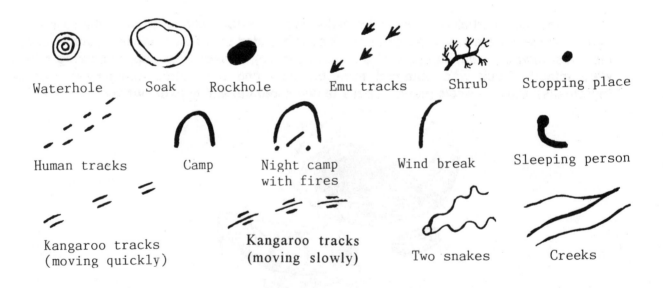

Waterhole Soak Rockhole Emu tracks Shrub Stopping place

Human tracks Camp Night camp with fires Wind break Sleeping person

Kangaroo tracks (moving quickly) Kangaroo tracks (moving slowly) Two snakes Creeks

Some symbols

Playing The Didgeridoo - Lesson 4.

To work on the techniques of this lesson, it is not necessary to be able to circular breathe. If you cannot yet circular breathe, don't let this deter you from attempting these techniques, because as you do, and as you carry out the following instructions carefully, this may just have you circular breathing where other ways of explanation, for you, did not succeed.

Rhythms And Rhythm Patterns

We are going to learn some ways of producing **rhythms**, and setting up **rhythm patterns**.

1.   (a) Instead of one long, continuous droning note, do a stop-start sound like a slow-firing machine gun. You can do this by mouthing a sound like 'Pa, Pa, Pa, Pa' etc., at the rate of about four bursts per second. Without using your voice, do this until you can produce a good, clear, regular set of notes, without stopping, for about 10 seconds (all on one breath).

(b) Now do only two notes as above and continue the second note (using the air in your cheeks) as you breathe in through your nose i.e. you circular breathe. The sound you mouth is like 'Pa Pa oom, Pa Pa oom', etc. <u>You may be able to learn to circular breathe if you work on this.</u>

The following may explain it better for you:

```
    o   o   i   o   o   i   o   o   i   o   o   i
Pa-Pa-oom-Pa-Pa-oom-Pa-Pa-oom-Pa-Pa-oom....
(Count)1           2           3           4
```

(<u>o</u> = blow out through your mouth)
(<u>i</u> = sniff in through your nose)
(<u>i</u> also means that you force air out of your cheeks)

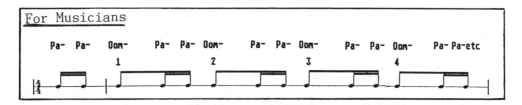

This will set up a good rhythm as you circular breathe in on every beat (or count). It should be at about marching time, but practice getting faster and faster.

Still having trouble circular breathing ?

Here is an easy exercise you can practise at any time, without the didgeridoo :

Breathe out through your mouth with your mouth in the shape it is when you say 'Aar', but don't make a sound. Now change your mouth to the shape it is when you say 'Ooo', still without making a sound. Do this several times and then, each time you mouth 'Ooo', breathe in through your nose. The changes in your mouth shape should now be as they are while you circular breathe.

(c) Let's do a similar thing to (b) above, but this time with three blown notes instead of two. It should be mouthed as 'Pa Pa Pa oom'.... or like 'Pa Pa Pa ooma'..... As above, you breathe in on 'oom'. Check out the following to get it right:

```
     o   o   o   i     o   o   o   i
    Pa-Pa-Pa-ooma-Pa-Pa-Pa-ooma....
     1       2   3       4
```

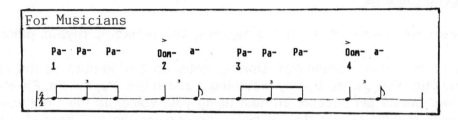

This sets up a slower rhythm pattern.

Try to figure out for yourself a rhythm pattern like those above, but beginning with four short blown notes.

2. **(a)** Start the drone note going and when you are ready, circular breathe in as you start to mouth sounds like 'Wonka Wonka Wonka'.... This pattern can be played without circular breathing, but as before, try to circular breathe on this, if you still haven't mastered it.

The following may help:

```
                        i   o   i   o   i   o   i   o
Drone first then :      Wonka-Wonka-Wonka-Wonka.....
                        1       2       3       4
```

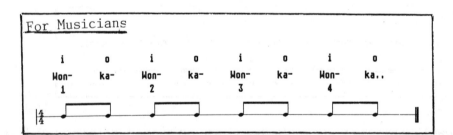

(b) Let's do a slower pattern based on 2(a). Start your drone going and then try mouthing the following sounds, 'Wonka-Wonkaaah-Wonka-Wonkaaah'...., breathing in (through your nose) on the 'Wonk' sound as you use air from your cheeks. On the 'a' and 'aaah' sounds you blow (using air from your lungs). Check out the following:

```
                        i   o   i   o.....i   o   i   o...
Drone first then:       Wonka-Wonkaaah-Wonka-Wonkaaah-.....
                        1   2   3   1       2   3
```

Notice that this is in three-four time (or waltz time).

(c) A slight modification of 2(b), also in three-four time, can be achieved by mouthing the 'Wonka' sound and extending the second syllable for two beats. It now is played as 'Wonkaaaah-Wonkaaaah'....... This is how you do it:

Drone first then:

```
         i  o......i  o.....
     Wonkaaaah-Wonkaaaah-....
     1   2   3   1   2   3
```

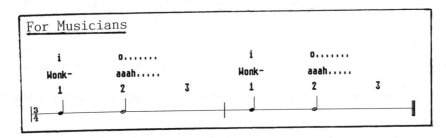

**(d) Now let us try something a little more complex. As in the above examples, start the drone note going and then mouth a sound like 'Wonka-Wonka-WaggaWagga-Wonka'.....
(Pronounce *Wagga* as Wogga.)**

The following should explain it:

```
  i   o   i  o.............i   o   i   o   i  o.............i   o
Wonka-Wonka-WaggaWagga-Wonka-Wonka-Wonka-WaggaWagga-Wonka ....
  1     2     3         4    1     2     3         4
```

This is done at about marching time. Notice that you continue to blow as you mouth the 'WaggaWagga' sound.

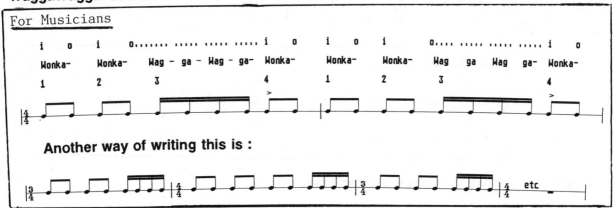

3. Double-Breathing Rhythm Patterns

With some rhythm patterns, you can take two quick breaths one after the other as you circular breathe. These patterns, as well as being interesting in themselves, are useful as rhythm changes, as well as being very helpful for recovering your breath after having done notes involving a lot of breathing out - such as a long series of voiced sounds or a single, long, voiced sound.

(a) These two patterns are in three-four time and can be played by working on the following:

```
        i    i    o    i    i    o    i    i
(i)   Wonk-Wonk-aah-Wonk-Wonk-aah-Wonk-Wonk-etc...
        1    2    3    1    2    3    1    2 ....
```

(ii)

```
   o    i    i    o    i    i    o    i
  Aah-Wonk-Wonk-Aah-Wonk-Wonk-Aah-Wonk-etc...
   1    2    3    1    2    3    1    2 ...
```

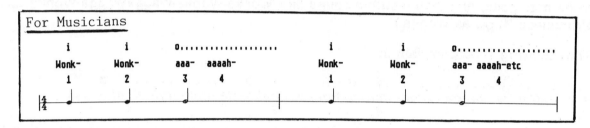

(b) These next two similar patterns are in four-four time. Work them out from the following:

(i)

```
     i    i    o.......i    i    o......
    Wonk-Wonk-aaaaah-Wonk-Wonk-aaaaah-etc...
     1    2    3    4   1    2    3    4 ...
```

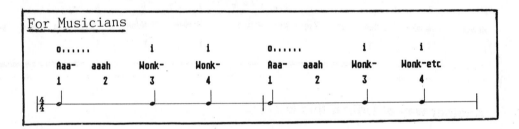

(ii)

```
   o.......i    i    o.......i    i
  Aaaaah-Wonk-Wonk-Aaaaah-Wonk-Wonk-etc...
   1    2    3    4    1    2    3    4 ...
```

For Musicians

Play these last two at about marching time.

Variations on these patterns can be worked out by changing tones as you mouth the 'aaaah' sounds in any of the above four exercises.

By combining the techniques covered in this lesson, and with practice, initiative and creativity, you should be able to discover for yourself a vast range of rhythms and rhythmic patterns. These will help give your playing colour and interest.

More About Circular Breathing

If you are having trouble circular breathing, try this:

During a short drone and while still droning, shape your mouth as if saying, 'Ooom'. Do not use your voice. As you mouth 'Ooom', take air in through your nose. Your drone may stop. This does not matter. Keep repeating this until the 'drone-ooom's merge together. Do this in front of a mirror and you should notice that as you mouth 'ooom' your cheeks cave inwards - this is when you sniff air in through your nose.

Practice, practice, practice.

CHAPTER 5

The Didgeridoo was and is used as an accompliment to chants and songs both for camp corroborees, where everyone joins in, and also for sacred ceremonies where only initiated males are allowed to participate. Sometimes special instruments are used, and these didgeridoos are engraved and/or painted and carefully stowed away for future use, whenever the group moves away to other areas. Some of these may be up to four metres long. Didgeridoos vary in pitch from as high as G to lower than A.

Didgeridoos are also used as solo instruments, maybe accompanied by clap sticks (rhythm sticks, click sticks), or boomerangs struck together, or by the hitting of the thighs with an open or cupped hand. Stamping of feet, sometimes augmented by the rustling of leaves tied around the ankles of dancers, also provides rhythm for the didgeridoo player. Hissing sounds, made by dancers or onlookers, also can provide interesting backing.

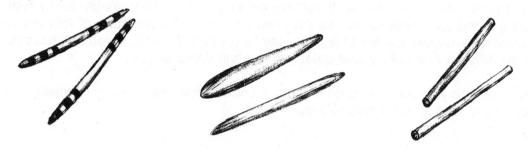

Clapping Sticks (click sticks; clap sticks: rhythm sticks)

Didgeridoo players in the past, as at present, would play for fun and for the entertainment of others, creating solo performances to display their virtuosity. At other times, especially when other groups were visiting on ceremonial occasions, didgeridoo players would take turns to keep the drone going all night to sooth the people of the tribe to sleep.

Other musical instruments used by the aborigines were often made for only temporary use. Of course boomerangs did not have to be made when a corroboree or ceremony was to be held. These hunting weapons make very effective percussion instruments. On the other hand, clap sticks can be very quickly made with a minimum of effort and, after use, can be used as fire wood. Clap sticks, made from woods specially selected for their resonant qualities and more carefully shaped, on the other hand, would sometimes be decorated by graving or painting, and these would be stored for future use.

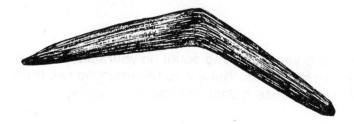

Boomerang: two are struck together, or one is used to hit the didgeridoo, to produce rhythm.

Playing The Didgeridoo - Lesson 5.

In this lesson we are going to combine some of the techniques we have covered so far, with the intention of making our rhythm patterns more interesting.

In modern solo playing and in using the didgeridoo as part of a band, it is important to be able to control when and where you add sounds such as barks, yells, howls, tone changes, and so on. These should not distract from your rhythm but enhance it. You should not clash with someone else's part, nor cover it . It is no good doing a great sound if it is not heard because it is poorly placed - better to add it at the end of a phrase in the music so that it is audible. In other words, do not just play haphazardly with no thought of what is happening with the rest of the music, and what is coming next; play and practice with a plan.

If you do not have your circular breathing going yet, it is still possible to do many of the following techniques without it. Like the previous lesson, some parts of this lesson can help to improve your circular breathing, or may help you to learn it, if you still have not managed to do it. Keep at it calmly and quietly and it will come to you.

1. Here we are going to yelp or bark (or do any other sound which has only one syllable and takes only one beat) on various beats in a bar.

(a) First Beat

(i) Start the drone going and hit your thigh with your hand to the count of four, 'One two three four, One two three four', etc. at a rate of about march time. Emphasize the first beat of every bar, i.e. each time you count 'One'.

(ii) On the first beat (each time you count 'One', in your mind), use your voice to shout a short, sharp 'Oo' (rhymes with 'toe') into the mouthpiece. Do this until you find it easy.

(b) Second Beat

As in (a), as you drone, hit your thigh, but this time shout 'Oo' one beat after the emphasized beat - just after you think 'One'. As you hit your thigh, think the following: One two three four, One Oo three four, One Oo three four, etc. In other words, you are making the 'Oo' sound on each second beat of the four beat bar. Practice it until you can do it easily.

(c) Third Beat

As above, drone, slap your thigh and count (in your mind) to four, emphasizing beat one, but now shout 'Oo' on beat three. Think it as follows: One two three four, One two Oo four, One two Oo four, etc. Practice it until you can do it easily.

(d) Fourth Beat

As above, drone, slap your thigh and count (in your mind) to four, emphasizing beat one, but this time shout 'Oo' on beat four. Think it this way: One two three four, One two three Oo, One two three Oo, etc. Practice it.

(e) First and Third Beats

As above, drone, slap your thigh and count (in your mind) to four, emphasizing beat one but now shout 'Oo' on beats one and three. Think it like this: <u>One</u> two three four, <u>Oo</u> two <u>Oo</u> four, <u>Oo</u> two Oo four, etc. Give it some practice.

(f) Second and Fourth Beats

As above, drone, slap your thigh and count (in your mind) to four, emphasizing beat one, this time shouting 'Oo' on beats two and four. This is the way to think it: <u>One</u> two three four, <u>One</u> Oo three Oo, <u>One</u> Oo three Oo, etc. Practice until you find it easy.

(g) First and Second, Second and Third, and Third and Fourth Beats

Good variations can be achieved by shouting 'Oo' on these beats. Use the above method to figure out for yourself how they can be produced. Practice these once you have figured them out.

(h) Other one-syllable sounds can be made instead of 'Oo' in the exercises above, and you can use high or low sounds, normal voice or falsetto. You can make sounds of two or even more syllables as well, if you time it right. To do this it is often easier to put the last syllable of the sound on the beat you are aiming for. For example, if you are going to make an 'Oo-Oo' sound near beat four, you think: <u>One</u> two three-and four, <u>One</u> two three-Oo-Oo, etc. Similarly, if you want to do 'Oo-Oo-Oo' near the fourth beat, you think, <u>One</u> two three-and-a four, <u>One</u> two three-Oo-Oo-Oo, etc. You will notice that here the last 'Oo' always hits on the fourth beat, the one we want in this case. If you wanted it to hit on beat two, you would have to think beat one as one-and-a, so that a three syllable sound like Oo-Oo-Oo would be thought of as <u>One</u>-Oo-Oo-Oo three four, etc.   Because the three 'Oo' sounds are so close together, to make them come out as separate notes, you should shout them as 'Toe' or 'Koe'.

(i) Syncopated Rhythms

When you emphasize normally unaccentuated beats, you produce syncopated rhythms. Syncopation is commonly used in jazz and rock'n'roll. The simplest example of this is when we emphasize the second and third beats, as we did in (f) above. A slightly more difficult example is achieved when we put the accent half a beat after each count. Let's put a shout on these accents, as follows: One-<u>and</u> two-<u>and</u> three-<u>and</u> four-<u>and</u>, One-<u>oo</u> two-<u>oo</u> three-<u>oo</u> four-<u>oo</u>,etc.

Try this:

One-<u>and</u> <u>two-and</u> three <u>four</u>, One-<u>oo</u> <u>oo-oo</u> three <u>oo</u>, etc.

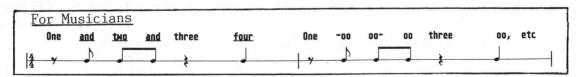

There are endless ways of adding syncopated accents when you insert sounds into rhythm patterns. Invent some of your own. Remember, any sound can be used instead of the 'oo's above.

If this has you confused or if it sounds too complicated, don't fret about it, just listen to how other players put their sounds in, and copy what you hear and like.

2. We are now going to <u>insert some sounds into a rhythm pattern without changing the rhythm</u>.

(a) One Syllable

(i) Look back to Lesson 4 and start up the rhythm pattern based on **Pa-Pa-Oom-Pa-Pa-Oom-etc.** Start this rhythm going and clap your thigh to keep the beat.

(ii) We are now going to use our voices to shout 'Oo' into this rhythm pattern without disrupting the overall rhythm. To do this look carefully at the following:

```
Pa-Pa-Oom-Pa-Pa-Oom-Pa-Pa-Oom-Pa-Pa-Oo,  Pa-Pa-Oom-}etc
     1            2            3            4            1
```

In this we shout 'Oo' in place of the 'Oom' mouthed on beat 4.

Practice until you can keep a good, steady rhythm going with loud 'Oo's on beat 4. Once you can do this, try it at different speeds. Also try making different one-syllable sounds, high, low, falsetto, etc.

(b) Two Syllables Clap and do the basic rhythm pattern as in (a) but this time, shout 'Oo-Oo' as shown in the following:

```
Pa-Pa-Oom-Pa-Pa-Oom-Pa-Pa-Oom-Oo-Oo-Pa-Pa-Oom-}etc.
     1            2            3      4            1
```

Now the 'Oo-Oo' takes the place of Pa-Pa-Oom on 'and-four' if you count 1 2 3 and 4, 1 2 3 and 4, etc.
Practice this as in (a) with variations in sounds and speeds.

(c) Three Syllables

(i) Do as in (b), but this time do a quick three syllables of 'Oo-Oo-Oo' instead of two to replace the Pa-Pa-Oom on 'and-four'. This has to be done quickly to fit in, but can be done with practice - to separate the sounds, pronounce them as 'toe' or 'koe'. Think of it this way as you count: 1 2 3 and-a-4. You shout 'Oo-Oo-Oo' on 'and-a-4'. After you've got it, practice with variations in sound and speed.

(ii) Do as in the above exercises but now do a slower three syllables of 'Oo-Oo-Oo' on beats (counts) 3 and 4, like this:

```
Pa-Pa-Oom-Pa-Pa-Oom-Pa-Oo-Oo-Oo-Pa-Pa-Oom-}etc.
     1            2      3   4         1
```

(d) Four Syllables Do the basic rhythm pattern and thigh clapping as above but now shout a four syllable 'Oo-Oo-Oo-Oo' on beats 3 and 4, counting three-and four-and, as follows:

```
Pa-Pa-Oom-Pa-Pa-Oom-Pa-Oo-Oo-Oo-Oo-Oom-Pa-Pa-Oom-}etc
     1            2      3      4            1
```

Once again, when you have figured it out, practice until it becomes easy for you: and then vary the sounds and speed.

(e) On the previous page, all of the sounds have been inserted into the rhythm pattern on beats 4 and sometimes 3 as well. You can put sounds on any of the beats if you want to. You can also syncopate the rhythm by inserting sounds off the beat. You do this by inserting the sound where we have 'Pa-Pa' instead of 'Oom'. Write these changes down as we did the others and then practice them.

3. This next exercise is a rhythm pattern in which we shall make some tone changes (like we shall do again in Lesson 6) and over which we shall <u>superimpose some voiced notes</u>.

Count this slowly, about half as fast as march time, and emphasize the sounds marked '>' as you drone and (without using your voice) shape your mouth as if to say the following:

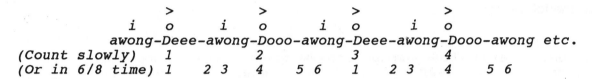

```
                              >            >            >            >
                 i      o      i      o      i      o      i      o
           awong-Deee-awong-Dooo-awong-Deee-awong-Dooo-awong etc.
(Count slowly)     1            2            3            4
(Or in 6/8 time) 1   2 3    4    5 6    1    2 3    4    5 6
```

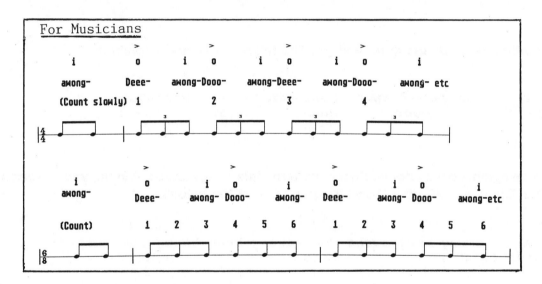

If we really emphasize the beat and over-do the tones on 'Deee' and 'Dooo', this piece will sound much more effective.

Now that we have practised this and can do it reasonable well, let's make it more interesting by adding an extra sound, while still continuing to do exactly what we were already doing. Impossible? Never.

(a) Do the above rhythm pattern, and as you do, use your normal speaking voice to make a sound like 'aaar' (as in car), each time you mouth 'Dooo'. The pitch of this superimposed note should be about the same as that of the drone note. If the pitch and the tone are right, you can get a growling effect where the added sound is not discernable. Emphasize beats 2 and 4. The following may help to explain:

```
                          >                       >
(Drone)      awong-Deee-awong-Dooo-awong-Deee-awong-Dooo-etc.
(Voice)                 aaar                    aaar
              1          2          3          4
```

(b) Do the rhythm pattern in its original form again, and then use your normal speaking voice to make a sound like 'eeer' (as in beer), each time you play 'Deee'. As in (a), the pitch should be approximately that of the drone note. This time emphasize beats 1 and 3. Check out the following:

```
                  >                       >
(Drone)      awong-Deee-awong-Dooo-awong-Deee-awong-Dooo-etc.
(Voice)          eeer                    eeer
              1          2          3          4
```

(c) Combine what we did in (a) and (b). The following should explain it:

```
                  >         >         >         >
(Drone)      awong-Deee-awong-Dooo-awong-Deee-awong-Dooo-etc.
(Voice)          eeer      aaar      eeer      aaar
              1          2          3          4
```

(d) Once again, do the original rhythm pattern. This time, instead of using your voice as you play the 'Dooo' sound, do a flutter tongue. Look at the following:

```
                          >                       >
(Drone)          awong-Deee-awong-Dooo-awong-Deee-awong-Dooo-etc.
(Flutter tongue)           trrr                    trrr
                  1          2          3          4
```

(e) Since to flutter tongue, you need to have your mouth and tongue shaped the same way as when you make an 'ooo' type sound, it is not possible (for me anyway) to flutter tongue on the 'Deee' part of the rhythm pattern. If however, you put the 'Dooo' before the 'Deee', that is on beats 1 and 3, and the 'Deee' on beats 3 and 4, you can do yet another variation. This may help:

```
                      >                       >
(Drone)          awong-Dooo-awong-Deee-awong-Dooo-awong-Deee-etc.
(Flutter tongue) trrr                    trrr
                  1          2          3          4
```

Experiment with the ideas we have dealt with in this lesson and you should be able to come up with new combinations of your own, or, if you put your mind to it, your own rhythm patterns and variations on these.

More About Double Notes.

If you play two notes (on any two instruments) which are exactly in tune, i.e. they are the same pitch, you should hear a pure, 'clean' sound. If you now alter one of the notes very slightly in pitch, you will hear, if you listen very carefully, a pulsing sound or beat. As you gradually increase the difference in pitch between the two notes, the speed of the pulse will increase - a discordant effect will be produced. This is what produces the growling effect on the didgeridoo when you sing a note nearly in the same pitch as the drone note. Try singing into the didgeridoo, a low note exactly the same pitch (or one or two octaves higher) as the drone note. Now slightly lower or raise the pitch of the note you are singing, and listen. You should hear a pulsing effect. Gradually lower or raise further, the note you are singing - the rate of pulsing will increase. Experiment with this phenomenon so that you can use it in your playing.

Eucalyptus miniata   (Darwin Woolybutt)

CHAPTER 6

The Didgeridoo Today

The didgeridoo has come from being an instrument used only in a few regions of Australia - Arnhem Land and the north-eastern Kimberleys - to become known in many parts of the world. It is now appreciated widely as a musical instrument, recognised and thought of as being, not only part of the Aboriginal culture in general, but as the origin of the sound which somehow typifies Australia - the natural environment - the bush, the landforms, the outback. It is a genuine part of Australia's heritage, just like the kangaroo, the platypus, wattles and gum trees, Uluru, the Great Barrier Reef, Aussie Rules, Sydney Harbour Bridge, Dame Nellie Melba, Albert Namatjira, lamingtons, and "Gidday Mate".

Once used only as a novelty by entertainers such as Rolf Harris, the didgeridoo now has wide acceptance as a serious instrument. Groups such as Gondwanaland and Yothu Yindi, and soloists such as Alan Dargin and David Hudson, have contributed to making this ancient instrument part of Australia's modern popular music, which is becoming known throughout the world.

Playing The Didgeridoo - Lesson 6.

In this lesson we are going to add to some of the topics covered in previous lessons, consolidate what we have discussed and played, and as well, touch on some new ideas.

1. Rhythm Patterns and Tone Changes

As well as adding colour and interest to your rhythm patterns by inserting, in appropriate places, sounds such as barks, yelps, and other animal calls, etc., we can also add tone changes which become part of the resulting pattern or theme. e.g.:

(a)

(i) Start up the rhythm pattern done previously where we mouthed 'Pa-Pa-Oom-Pa-Pa-Oom- etc.' and then add the tone change we did earlier on, when we changed from 'Ooo' to 'eee' while we droned, as shown here:

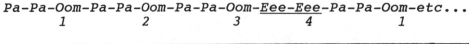

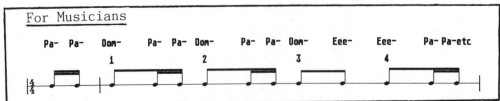

Try to make the 'Eee-Eee' sound very definite and nasal, so as to stand out and become part of the rhythm pattern. Remember, here we are not using our voices to make sounds, we are only shaping our lips, mouths and tongues as we drone. Practice this pattern until you can do it without thinking too hard.

(ii) Modify the above rhythm pattern so that you end up with a continuing, mouthed theme like this:

Pa-Pa-Oom-<u>Eee-Eee</u>-Pa-Pa-Oom-<u>Eee-Eee</u>-Pa-Pa-Oom-Pa-Pa-Oom-Pa-
   1   2   3   4   1   2

Pa-Oom-<u>Eee-Eee</u>-Pa-Pa-Oom-<u>Eee-Eee</u>-etc...
  3   4   1   4

Practice this until it becomes easy. You can modify this and invent new variations for yourself. You can also substitute any number of two-syllable sounds to replace all or some of the 'Eee- Eee' tones. In other words, explore the possibilities.

(b)

 (i) Produce the rhythm pattern we did in the previous lesson where we mouthed the sounds as, 'Wonka-Wonka- Wagga-Wagga-Wonka ' etc... Now modify it so it is done like this:

Wonka-Wonka-Wagga-Wonk-Eeeee-Wonka-Wonka-Wagga-Wonk-Eeeee-etc.
1   2 3   4 1   2   3   4

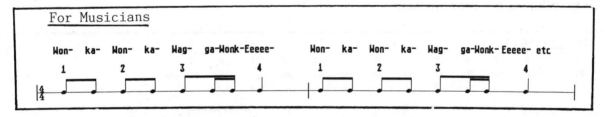

Practice this to make it easy.

(ii) Modify the pattern you have just done in (i) so that it is mouthed as the following:

Wagga-Wonk-Eeee-Wagga-Wonk-Eeee-Wonka-Wonka-Wagga-Wonk-Eeee-etc..
 1   2 3   4 1 2 3   4

As before, practice this until you have it easily, and then modify it into new patterns.

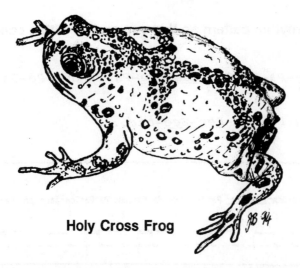

Holy Cross Frog

(c) One of Australia's most colourful frogs, the Holy Cross Frog (Notaden bennetti), and its three very close relatives from northern and central Australia, make rhythmic sounds which can be copied on the didgeridoo. After heavy rain, they dig up out of their burrows and the males set up a chorus as they call to attract the females. Copy the sound they make, as follows:

```
    o   i   o   o   i   o   o   i   o   o   i   o   i
    Ah-oo-ee-Ah-oo-ee-Ah-oo-ee-Ah-oo-ee-Ah...
        1           2           3           4
```

The 'Ah' sound has a slightly lower pitch than the rest of the notes - this can easily be achieved on the didge.

The timing for this pattern is about half as fast as march time - fairly slow.
(i = breathe in; o = breathe out)

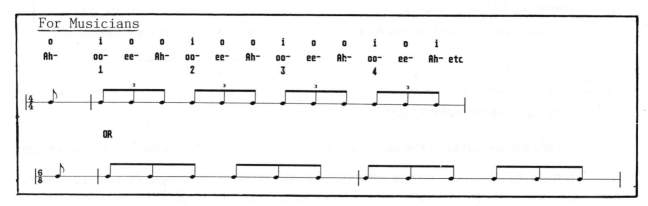

(d) A very effective method of creating rhythm patterns and also of producing some interesting sound variations is to hit your cheek with your hand as you play. In this way, air is forced out of your cheeks. Try it as you play various rhythm patterns.

2. Didgeridoo Languages.

If you listen to accomplished players, you will hear within their playing, what sounds like repeated phrases which the didgeridoo is saying. These are not words spoken by the actual voice of the player but sounds which come about as a result of how the tones are mouthed into the mouth-piece, especially while circular breathing is occurring. Often this 'language' is a means by which a particular player can be recognized. You will not hear this identifying sound pattern every time the didgeridooist (now there is a new word for the English language) plays - it depends on what is being played - but when the didge player is simply filling in between added sounds and featured fills, you will often discern this diagnostic pattern recurring.

In areas where didgeridoo is part of Aboriginal culture, certain styles ('languages') can be discerned which are predominant in particular regions. There may be several 'didgeridoo languages', usually related in technique, to be found in the one region.

However, different 'languages' are used for differing songs or pieces, depending on their purpose and the occasion of the performance, even when the same didgeridooist is playing. Listen for these languages when you hear other players. Copy them, and then develop your own unique style. If you play a lot, this will probably happen spontaneously, but being aware of this, you can help to make your playing more interesting and entertaining by directing the final shape of *your* languages.

Here are some much simplified 'languages', or parts thereof, of some players. Shape your lips and mouth, and position your tongue (without using your voice) to produce a patterned drone based on the following:

Diddawong-Diddawong-Wong-Diddawong-Diddawong-Diddawong-Wong-etc.

Liddle-Oh-Liddle-Oh-Lid-Liddle-Oh-Liddle-Oh-etc...

Dorm-De-Dorm-De-Dorm-Did-Dee-Dorm-Dorm-Dorm-De-Dorm-Dorm- etc...

Didgeridoo-Didgeridoo-Didgeri-Didgeri-Didgeridoo-etc...

Now, when you listen to the same players, you may not hear exactly what I have written down, but it will be something similar - copy what you think you hear.

Notice also that each of the above patterns (except the last one) do not have a regular bar by bar beat to which you can continue to count, 'One, two, three, four, One, two, etc.,' but you can keep a constant steady beat going while you play each. Try it while you belt your thigh in time. Though much of their music was often highly and complexly structured, Aborigines did not always use recurring bars of equal length.

In their sacred ceremonial music, traditional Aboriginal players used didgeridoo languages which were only performed for these special occasions and only heard by male initiates. They do not play these in public.

In regions where the didgeridoo was originally part of the musical and ceremonial tradition, only males played this instrument. Didgeridooists from elsewhere should respect this cultural requirement, if and when they are in these traditional areas.

3. Speaking Through The Didgeridoo.

Instead of just mouthing sounds or words, actual words can be spoken through the didgeridoo, and can be heard and understood. To do this, continue to drone and speak words, phrases or even whole sentences through the mouth-piece, using a falsetto voice. You can do this with your normal voice as well, but words do not always come out so clearly. Some words are easier to say and to be understood than others. This is because, to keep the didgeridoo droning, your lips have to be in a certain shape, and to speak certain words, you have to shape your lips in other ways. It is the same problem ventriloquists are faced with - they have to be able to say words without moving their lips. Practice will help. Try counting to one hundred while maintaining your drone. Also, try reciting poems or nursery rhymes during an extended drone.

It is possible to sing songs through the didgeridoo. This often works much better when you use a falsetto voice. It also works best when the song has fewer chords, otherwise it will not sound very musical.

Try sounding the 'Didgeridoo-Didgeridoo' etc.... 'language' (see above) through the didge while at the same time speaking the word 'didgeridoo' every second bar (4 beats) or so. You can do this in high, low or falsetto voices.

4. 'Horn' Notes or Overtones.

If you tighten your lips at just the right tension and blow, you should be able to produce a higher note on your didgeridoo. You may have to blow a little harder than normal at first, until you get used to it, and this 'hooted' note may sound something like a fog horn. You can produce a short, explosive sound on the horn note by 'tongueing' it - i.e. put your tongue out to a position between your lips and then do what you do when you spit something off the end of your tongue - in fact, if you are not careful, this is exactly what you will do. You can also produce this 'spat' overtone by a spitting action using just the tightened lips. This 'horn' note is usually a 10th above the basic drone note for your instrument, or it may be higher or lower, depending on your didgeridoo, but the sound can be put to good effect in various ways. For example:

(a) The spat overtone can be used as a kind of punctuation mark - like a comma within a sentence or as a full-stop at the end of a performance.

(b) The spat horn note and longer hooted horn note can be used as a part of a performance just as another sound, as you would with a yelp, bark, or 'wok, wok' sound, etc., to provide variation and interest.

(c) You can use either the spat overtone or the hooted overtone as part of a rhythm pattern, using them to replace other sounds we have put into these. Go back to some of these and try them, this time doing a short horn note (or notes) instead of the sounds we used in the original versions.

(d) The spat horn note can be used to produce a drum-like effect, to become the main part of a rhythm pattern. This is where it is probably best to 'tongue' it, though alternatively, it can be blown normally with tightened lips, if you use your diaphragm to give a quick burst of air.

(i) Make a short , sharp 'Tump' sound on the horn note, and then produce a drone which sounds like 'Oo-wah-da' , make another tongued 'Tump' horn note, leave a one-beat space and then start all over again. The following may help to explain it:

```
(Horn)          i  (Horn)        (Horn)         i  (Horn)
Tump  Oo-wah-da  Tump  (space)  Tump  Oo-wah-da  Tump  (space)  etc...
  1        2        3       4      1        2        3       4
```

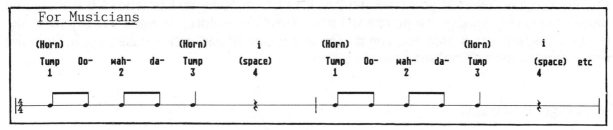

You can vary this by putting another horn note in the space.

(ii) You can make a longer and more complex pattern as follows:

```
(Horn)          i  (Horn)         i  (Horn)          i  (Horn)           i
Tump  Oo-da-wah  Tump  Oo-ah-wap  Tump  Oo-da-wah  Tump  Oo-ah-wap  etc.
  1        2        3        4       1        2        3        4
```

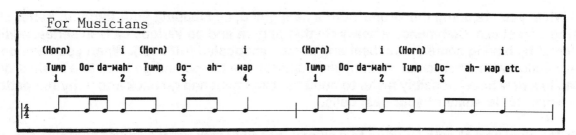

You can invent other patterns of your own, if you play around with these and similar sounds.

(e) If you practice hard, you can even treat the horn note as you would the drone note, and circular breathe on it. In fact you can do many of the tone changes and rhythm producing effects that you can when playing on the drone note. You can even produce a higher 'horn' note to go with this much higher pitched playing style. These overtones are easier to use with a didgeridoo of lower pitch. Theoretically at least, you can even play and circular breathe on this higher horn note as well, and so on, ad infinitum. At present though, leave all this for the future.

5. Clap Sticks.

Clap sticks can be used to enhance the sound of the didgeridoo. A couple of short pieces of hard wood about 25 to 35 centimetres long will suffice. While playing the didge, lie one on your lap and strike it with the other, but be careful what you hit. You can also hold one clap stick in the hand holding the didgeridoo, while hitting it with the clap stick in the other hand.

Another way to achieve a clap stick effect is to use only one thin stick, about a centimetre diameter and about 30 to 40 centimetres long. This is used to hit the didgeridoo as you play. You may not want to use this method if your didgeridoo is a work of art.

6. Didgeridoo Solos

You may be busking, doing a spot at a cabaret, doing a didgeridoo demonstration, playing at a party, soloing in a band number, or simply amusing yourself, but whatever it is, you will want to produce a solo which has _variation_ (so it doesn't become boring), sounds _creative_ (even if you have worked it out previously and practiced it a thousand times) and is _entertaining_ - so people will say, "Wow". Therefore, so you are ready when the time comes, prepare a solo you can do (apparently ad libbed) when called upon. Here are some suggestions on putting some together:

(a) A Progressive Solo.

(i) Start with a basic drone with no tempo (i.e. no apparent beat). Add some tone changes (you know - 'Ooee' etc.) and don't hurry, followed by some 'Wok-Wok' sounds. Add just a couple of quiet and under-stated rhythm patterns as you circular breathe, then do a few low and quiet animal calls (e.g. Boobook Owls etc.) with some sounding up close and others answering from far away. Maybe you could then do a call (it does not have to be particular animal) that is up close, loud and trailing away into the distance, to lead you back into a drone with no tempo.

(ii) While you are doing this drone, start a beat going, by slapping your thigh or, better still, using clap sticks. Commence a heavy rhythm pattern and do various calls in series, adding interest by having some on the beat and some syncopated (off beat). When you have done one section with a particular rhythm, you can drop the tempo and go back to a basic drone. Clap in a new beat - possibly faster to build the excitment and go back into a rhythm pattern on which to do some of your best calls.

(iii) The final part should build up to a climax, possibly with drama and/or humour. The end should be definite, for example with one or two short, sharp horn notes, so that the audience is left in no doubt that you have finished, and therefore know when to applaud.

(b) A Solo Based on a Theme.

(i) Begin with a fundamental drone, possibly with added low voiced notes, and, after a few bars, go into an interesting rhythm pattern which is to be used as the theme.

(ii) Make the theme pattern more interesting by emphasizing one or more beats within it and/or by including tone changes - some very nasal.

(iii) Add low voiced notes or chords to one or more beats in the pattern, but keep coming back after each alteration to the original theme.

(iv) Occasionally, suspend the rhythm and hold a loud droned note with an added low voiced sound with or without a tongue flutter. Return continually to the theme.

(v) Finish by adding an emphasized beat at the end of one of the suspended drones as in step(iv)

(c) <u>A Solo Based On A Tempo</u>.

This is somewhat like the Theme Solo but here you do variation after variation, while keeping to a particular tempo. David Hudson's "Didgerijig" (see Discography on the last page of this book) is a good example.

A couple of important points about solos:

● Make sure your solo is <u>*not too long*</u>. Leave them wanting more. Quit while you're ahead.

● Have a definite <u>*start, a body and an end*</u> to your solo.

● Have <u>*light and shade*</u> in your act. i.e. soft parts and loud parts, slow parts and fast parts. If a band is backing you, you may have to keep their tempo, or conduct them to change tempo.

● Don't show all your tricks - keep some in reserve. You may have to do an <u>*encore*</u>. Have two or more solos worked out, in case.

● Unless you are in a small room, it is a definite advantage to <u>*amplify*</u> the didgeridoo. The didge sounds great when played into a microphone and through an amplifier or sound system. The mike should be placed just in front of the opening - not your end, Silly. An acoustic method of amplifying the didgeridoo is to place the end on a table, bench-top, etc., or place it on a metal bucket or drum. You could even make yourself a small resonating chamber - something like an acoustic guitar body. The Aborigines used to use large baler shells in the same way.

7. Playing to a Musical Backing.

You may be in a band or have the opportunity of being backed by a band; or you may be able to back yourself on the guitar or keyboards (you have to figure out a method of holding the didge steady while you do this). The first thing you have to know is what key your didgeridoo is in. A long didge may give a basic note of B♭ (very low, or even lower), B, C, C♯ or D. Shorter ones will sound an E♭, E or F, F♯, G, G♯, A or even higher. Ones in C sharp (D flat), or F sharp (G flat) are a problem in that not many songs tend to be written or played in these keys - but it can be done by any good musician.

If your didgeridoo is a quarter of a tone off any of these notes, you have a bigger problem. You can change the pitch up or down as you play if you have a good ear - and with some didgeridoos this is easier than with others - or you can raise the pitch permanently by cutting a little off your instrument - the didge, Silly. But this is fraught with danger, and should be attempted only by an experienced and skilled didgeridoo maker. Even so, some of the art work may have to go. The other alternative is to play, forever flat or sharp, which is not a problem when playing solo, or if the other players tune to your didge.

Since the didgeridoo plays basically only one note, there is a limit to the type of music for which it is appropriate. The fewer the chord changes the better. This problem has, to an extent, been overcome with the invention of the 'didgeribone' - a didgeridoo made of two pieces of P.V.C. pipe that slide into each other - but this is getting away from tradition. Having a variety of didgeridoos in various keys is also a way of overcoming the fact that music is played in different keys.

In spite of the limitations mentioned, there is still plenty that can be done with the didgeridoo as an instrument used with other pitched instruments.

For example:

(i) Some pieces have only one chord, or a couple of chords. Here there is no problem - so long as the chord in the backing has the didge note in it, it will be in harmony with it. For example, a D didge will sound okay against the following chords because they all have a D note in them - D, B minor, G, A suspended fourth, E minor seventh, E seventh, C ninth, etc.

(ii) Some chords without the didge note in them will also harmonize and sound okay so long as the note played by the didgeridoo is one of a number of notes in the scale of the chord being played. For example, if the chord is C, the third note of the C scale (namely E) and the fifth (G) will sound good with it. In other words, a C didgeridoo, a G didgeridoo or an E would sound right when played against a C chord. The fourth note (F in the C scale) and the sixth note (A in C) will also harmonize with the tonic chord (named by the first note of the scale - C in the scale of C - C chord). You see therefore, the didgeridoo can be played all through some songs even though the chords are changing; so long as the chords are the right ones.

I will illustrate some music which will sound appropriate with the didgeridoo. All examples will be in the key of D - you would use a D didge for these. If you do not have a D didgeridoo and know no music theory, don't worry, any musician will understand what key to play in and can transpose the backing to suit your didge.

12 Bar Blues

This is the chord progression for backing most blues numbers and many rock'n'roll songs. Here are the chords to play to accompany the didge, or for the musos to back you. Remember, if you do not have a D didgeridoo, you will have to change the key. If you do not know what key yours is, have a musician play a note the same pitch as your didge plays. The name of that note is the key in which you have to have the backing played.

Didgeridoos Blues

‖:D |D |D |D7 |G7 |G7 |D |

|D |A7 |G7 |D |A7   :‖D |D   ‖

While these chords are being played, do a drone with rhythm patterns, fills and sounds, etc.

The didge (playing a D note) does not fit in with the A7 chord as well as with the others because there is no D in the A7 chord, but because D is the fourth note in the A scale, we get a A7sus4 chord when we play D against the A7, so we can get away with it.

Because the chords of G, C9 and D7 have the note D in them, you can also play a D didge right through a 12 Bar Blues sequence in the key of G.

Study in D for Didge

```
‖ :Em7     |Em7      |D        |D        |Em7      |Em7      |D        |
                *        *
|D        |Gma7     |Gma6     |D        |D        : ‖
```

*You may substitute A6 and G6 (= F#m7 & Em7) or Asus4 and A7 for these chords respectively.

To play this study, simply do a drone and add rhythm patterns with fills and sounds in appropriate places while these chords are being played.

On the next page you will find this study again, slightly modified and arranged for didgeridoo, rhythm guitar, and an instrument to play a melody line (e.g. keyboards, saxophone, another guitar, violin, etc.) Don't forget, when the melody is being played, it is often more effective to do dramatic sounds (such as yelps, 'wok's and so on) at the ends of phrases, rather than during them, unless it is within an accentuated part, such as in the two bars where the chords are Gma7 and Gma6.

This version of the study (on page 41), we'll call it 'D For Didge', should be played at a steady rate of about slow march time. The didgeridoo starts first with no backing, and here you do a basic drone with tone changes, but with no hint of a beat. When it comes in, the guitar keeps a steady rhythm going while the didgeridoo stays with tone changes in the background until the two bars in which the triplets are accentuated (i.e. on Gma7 and Gma6). Here it is appropriate to do some yelps, etc. as fills. In the next two bars you go back to a basic drone with tone changes. The melody line now starts, and here the didgeridoo should continue with the drone and tone changes, but at the end of phrases put in some suitable fills.

If the piece was to be done in jazz style, after the initial run through the melody, subsequent repeats would involve variations of the theme, usually with the various instruments taking turns at improvisation. When it is time for the didge (that's you; yes, YOU !) to improvise, then you can take the limelight and do some crazy fills. But don't go totally off the track. As you play, listen to the backing that the other musos are laying down for you and work around this. As you do this, think through the melody as you play, and try to add fills which fit in with the general theme of it. It would also be sensible in this situation not to play at all during some of the repeats - that is, when the other musicians are doing their things. Or, it might be an idea only to add a sound or two here and there without a continuous drone going. Understatement is sometimes better than over-kill. The last time through, in jazz, is usually more or less the straight melody again.

Eucalyptus tetrodonta   (Darwin Stringybark)

D for Didge

Music by John Bowden.

Learning From Live Performances

Listening to other players is very important in increasing your store of knowledge of didgeridoo tones, rhythm patterns, phrasing, added sounds and other ways of adding variety to your playing. This may also be a source of inspiration. Go to see as many live performances as possible. Most Aboriginal groups not only have didgeridoo players featured in their acts but also share interesting cultural information with their audiences. You may see and be entertained by Aboriginal performers in annual events at places such as Laura and Darwin. At Karanda, there is live theatre almost every day of the week. The Maleny Folk Festival and the BEMAC musical festival at Yungaba in Brisbane are other happenings where Aboriginal and non-Aboriginal players may be seen and heard. Information about these can be obtained from your local tourist bureau. Make these events part of the itinerary on your next trip north (or south) - you will be well rewarded. Some great players are only too happy to explain how they do things.

Learning From Recordings

Live performances, though invaluable experiences, are ephemeral - they happen and then are gone - you remember the act as a whole, but the finer details of the didgeridooist's technique have mostly escaped you or are forgotten. Recordings, on the other hand, are permanent reminders of what was played, and these can be used to enable you to figure out how particular sounds were achieved. At first, it might seem impossible to tell how the performer is accomplishing what is on the recording, but with experience you will find it a lot easier. The following are some hints to help you work out what is being played:

1. To figure out the basis of a rhythm pattern or a language, first play the part of the performance you want to copy, and then press the pause button. If the pattern is repeated on the recording, let this play before pausing it. Play this part many times and listen very carefully.

2. Try to put into words, the sounds you think are being mouthed to produce the overall pattern of tones you are hearing. What you hear may not be what someone else hears - this does not matter.

3. You must now determine where the player is blowing the sounds, and if, and exactly where, circular breaths are being taken. This is a very crucial consideration.

To detect where breaths are being inhaled, listen for sounds containing certain vowel sounds, such as '_ooo_' (as in do), '_oh_' (as in go) '_ooom_' (as in room), '_wha_' (as in what), '_ooh_' (as in wool) and '_oor_'(as in door). You will notice that to make these sounds, your lips are pushed forwards and in a pursed or rounded shape, and that your cheeks are concave (i.e. caved in). Your lips and cheeks move to these positions when you push air out of your mouth while you circular breathe. Now, you can make these same sounds as you blow as well, so where you hear them is not necessarily or always where a breath is being inhaled, but you can suspect that it might be.

Some sounds produced on the didgeridoo can only be made by blowing, and cannot be made as you breathe in through your nose (while you circular breathe). All voiced sounds (yelps, growls, howls, barks, coos, etc.), all flutter-tongued sounds and all doubled notes are a sure indication that the player is blowing the sound. We know therefore, that circular breaths are not being taken in during any of these sounds. We can therefore look elsewhere to find where to breathe in.

Most 'wok' sounds are done while blowing, but can also be made while circular breathing, so are not an infallible guide as to where to breathe in. A gravelly, or rough, growling sound may be the result of a low (usually), voiced, doubled note, or it could be a flutter-tongued note, and indicates that the player is blowing, not breathing in.

4. Write down the sounds, in words, which approximate what you hear, put the letter 'i' above the syllables that you have calculated the player breathed in, and then play what you have. Minor adjustments may be necessary to better approximate the recorded sounds. Remember to make allowances for the possibility that your didgeridoo may be of a different pitch to that of the player's, and is also likely to have a different basic tone.

5. Practise the copied sounds or pattern until you find it easy. Do this at every practice session until it has become part of your musical vocabulary. Come back and listen to the recording again some time later. You might find that you missed some subtleties the first time, that you may now pick up.

6. Make modifications to the original, copied sound until you have something new that is yours. Practice this until you can do it almost automatically.

By listening to recordings of many different didgeridoo players, and following the above procedures, you will be on your way to becoming a better player, with your own unique style.

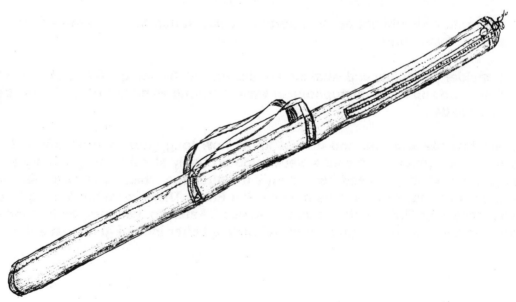

Didgeridoo Carry-bag of suede, cloth or leather

Selecting And Buying A Didgeridoo

Before buying it, you need to ask yourself, "*What do I want of a didgeridoo ?*"

The answer to this question will help you choose.

If you want it only as *a work of art*, to hang on the wall, or to put on display, then you should pick a didgeridoo that has the appearance you like. Consider the following:

● Those done in natural ochre colours - browns, reds, yellows, earthy pinks and mauves, black and white - look much more authentic than those in ornate, glossy hues.

● Remember, the more intricate the design, the more it will cost you - a lot of work goes into such decoration.

If you want a didgeridoo as *a playing instrument*, here are several points to give thought to:

● What **key** will be most useful? Do you want a deep (low pitched) note or a higher pitch?

● What basic **tonal qualities** do you prefer? This is a matter of personal taste. Play and listen carefully to the instrument before you buy, or have someone else play.

● If you are playing with a band or another musician, or accompanying yourself, a didgeridoo in C, D or E will be suitable; but make sure it is on the note, not slightly higher or lower. Maybe, if you can afford it, you should buy a selection of didges of different keys. Or buy just one wooden one; and several decorated P.V.C. ones in useful keys, or make yourself a 'didgeribone'.

● Be certain that the size of the blowing end suits you - that it is not too small or too large. A mouth-piece can make up for an opening which is a little large.

● Decoration should not be an important consideration here, it is ease of playing, and sound that counts.

● Consider portability and what kind of act you will be doing. Will you have to hold the didgeridoo up to the microphone or wave it around all night? A hernia may be a thing to consider.

If **you are just starting out**, and do not know how long your interest will last, or what success you are going to have as a player, you probably should not spend a great deal of money just yet. What you need here then is a didgeridoo which is easy to play, light and portable, looks good, and yet does not cost the Earth. There is no such thing? Yes, there is. A well-decorated P.V.C. didge is what you need. Later on, you may wish to move on up to a wooden instrument - and then you will have a better idea of just what suits you best.

Taking Care Of Your Didgeridoo

Regardless of what kind of didgeridoo you have, it needs to be taken care of. With proper care it will last a life time and more. To this end, the following suggestions should be noted:

● Never leave a didgeridoo out in the sun. The bees wax of the mouth-piece will melt - but this is a minor problem. Much more importantly, a wooden didgeridoo is liable to warp and split. A didgeridoo that has been made from a tree that was living when it was cut, should have been well-seasoned before it was finished off and sold. One made from dead timber, that had been dead some time before being processsed, would have been well cured naturally, and should be therefore less likely to split - but do not take risks by leaving a didge out in the weather. Some timbers are more prone to splitting than others.

● If you wet the inside of a didgeridoo before you play it, this seems to enhance its tone and volume. But do not soak it in water for any length of time - you will, once again, be tempting fate. Absorption of water by the wood may cause expansion, and with later drying out, contraction. This may lead to splitting.

● If you wish to change the shape of the wax mouth-piece, simply warm it for a short time to make it pliable. Bees wax is susceptible to wax moth larvae, which bore small holes through it and leave cobweb trails on the outside. If this happens, it does not matter much, unless the infestation is destroying the mouth-piece altogether, in which case you may need to take the whole thing off, melt it down in a warm frying pan or other suitable container, and after it has solidified, mould it onto the didgeridoo again. If you know a bee keeper, ask for some spare wax - the darker stuff that beekeepers call 'slum gum' seems to be less liable to attack.

● If you have need to carry your didgeridoo around, and you value it, you could have a carry bag made, as you would for any valuable instrument. A bag with padded compartments would be useful if you needed to carry several.

Multi-compartment Carry-bag
for didgeridoos

Bibliography and Further Study

The following are a few of the many books which relate to Aboriginal culture. There are many more available. Also included are some books on forest trees and Australian birds.

An Illustrated Encylopaedia Of Aboriginal Life.
A. W. Reed.   J W Books Pty. Ltd. Brookvale,N. S. W., 1974.

Australian Aboriginal Culture.
Australian InFo International.   A G P S Press, Canberra, 1989.

Australian Dreaming. 40,000 Years Of Aboriginal History.
Jennifer Isaacs.   Lansdowne Press, Sydney, 1986.

Aboriginal Pathways In Southeast Queensland And The Richmond River.
J.G. Steele.   University of Queensland Press, 1984.

Before The Whiteman. Aboriginal Life In Prehistoric Australia.
Readers Digest, 1974.

[1,2] Forest Trees of Australia.
N. Hall, R. Johnson, G. Chippendale.   A G P S, Canberra, 1975.

From Earlier Fleets - Hemisphere - An Aboriginal Anthology.
Ed. R. Henderson.   Curriculum Development Centre, 1989.

Nomads Of The Australian Desert.
Charles E. Mountford.   Rigby Pty. Ltd., Adelaide, 1976.

The Rainbow Serpent.
Oodgeroo Noonuccal and Kabul Noonuccal.   A G P Press, Canberra, 1988.

Field Guide To The Birds Of Australia.
K. Simpson and N. Day.   Viking O'Neil, Penguin Books, Australia, 1986

The Queensland Aborigines   Vols 1, 2, 3
W.E. Roth.   Heperian Press. Facsimile Ed., 1984

The Slater Field Guide To Australian Birds.
P. Slater, P. Slater and R. Slater.   Rigby, 1986.

Tom Petrie's Reminiscences Of Early Queensland.
C.P. Campbell Petrie.   University of Queensland Press, 1992

Voices Of The First Day - Awakening In The Aboriginal Dreamtime
R. Lawlor.   Inner Traditions, Rochester, Vermont, 1991

Discography

The following are just a few of the many fine recordings of Aboriginal music, and music featuring the didgeridoo. Also included is a recommended bird-call tape.

<u>Arnhem Land Vol. 1</u>.   EMI 1956 Recorded by A. P. Elkin.

<u>Arnhem Land Vol. 2</u>.   EMI 1956 Recorded by A. P. Elkin.

<u>Arnhem Land</u>.   The A.P. Elkin Collection, Larrikin Records. 1993

<u>Bird Calls Of Eastern Australia</u>.   Len Gillard.
          Gillard Bird Cassettes, Prospect, Tasmania. 1988.

<u>Bloodwood. The Art of Didgeridoo</u>.   Alan Dargin with Michael Atherton.
          Natural Symphonies. 1991.

<u>Budal Lardil</u>.   Songs of Mornington Island.   Larrikin Records, 1993

<u>Didgeridoo Dreaming</u>.   Alistair Black, Larrikin Records, 1992

<u>Gondwanaland</u>.   Gondwanaland.   Warner Bros. Music. 1987.

<u>Kakadu.</u>   Tony O'Connor.   Steve Parish Publishing. 1992.

<u>Mark Atkins Plays Didgeridoo</u>.   Mark Atkins, Enrec., 1992

<u>Music of My People. Australian Aboriginal Music</u>
Presented by Bob Maza.   Twin Track Productions.

<u>Proud To Be Aborigine</u>.   Tjapukai Dancers, Jarra Hill Records, 1990

<u>Travelling Songs</u>.   Gondwana, ABC Music, 1994

<u>Wildlife</u>.   Gondwanaland.   W E A. 1989.

<u>Woolunda, Ten Solos For Didgeridoo</u>.   David Hudson.   Celestial Harmonies. 1993.

<u>Playing The Didgeridoo</u> - a complete course.   John Bowden. 1995

available from the author - P.O. Box 508 Kallangur, Queensland 4503, Australia.

A Final Word

Success at any learning comes back ultimately to the student. Those who will gain most from this book will be those who make the most effort and put in the most time. Natural talent is the other variable, but, without dedication, this will not help much. On the other hand, time and effort will greatly reward the person of average natural ability. Give it all you have.

Best of luck.

NOTES

NOTES

NOTES